A Guide to Keith Johnstone's
MAESTRO IMPRO™

Cover Photograph:
Picnic Improvisación Teatral
Monkey Fest
Bogota, Colombia
by Fernanda Pineda

Published 2019 by the International Theatresports™ Institute (ITI)

215 - 36 Avenue NE, Unit 6 | Calgary, AB | T2E 2L4 | CANADA

Copyright© 2019 ITI

This guide is in no way a replacement for performance rights.
Non performance rights holders wishing to perform the Maestro Impro™ format should apply at:
admin@theatresports.org.

Layout: Dagmar Bauer konzipiert & gestaltet, Stuttgart, Germany
Illustrations by Haley Brown, haleybrown.org

»The best Directors are those who know innately how to inspire their partners. They have strong storytelling skills.« *Shawn Kinley*

CONTENTS

8 INTRODUCTION
8 About This Guide
8 Keith Johnstone
9 The International Theatresports™ Institute (ITI)
9 Before Playing Maestro Impro™

10 MAESTRO IMPRO™ BACKGROUND
10 What is Maestro Impro™?
10 Maestro Origins
10 The Name
12 Maestro Around the World
12 What Maestro Can Achieve

14 IMPORTANT CONCEPTS
14 How Maestro is Unique
14 The Spirit
15 Risk and Failure
15 Teamwork
16 Skills

18 PREPARATION
18 What You Need for Maestro
18 The Scoreboard
19 Pinnies/Buttons
19 Coins/Bowls
19 Duration
19 The Space
19 Placement of the Directors
20 Before the Show
20 Warm-up Class
21 Pre-show Meeting

22 MAESTRO IN DETAIL
22 The Start of the Show
22 Sample Opening
22 The Emcee and Scorekeeper
23 Voting/Scoring
25 Scene Rounds
25 Lightning Rounds
26 Eliminations
26 Directors
26   Who Should Direct
27   Responsibility
27   Challenges
28   Who and When to Direct
28   Preparation for Directing
29   Choosing the Players
29   Awareness of the Players
29   Variations and Practice
30   Player Initiative
30   Relationships
31   Questions/Triggers to Inspire Performers
31   Over-directing
34   Under-directing
34   New Directors
34   Summary of Directing Skills
35   Useful Directing
36 Players
36   Advice
36   Behaviour/Misbehaviour
37   Joining Scenes
37 Ending the Game
38 The Winner and Ending the Show
39 Sample Closing
39 The Prize

40 ATTENTION TO DETAIL
40 Content
40 Permission and Difficult Content
41 Fairness
41 Tips
42 Pitfalls
42 Scenography
43 Music
43 Lights and Sound

44 IN CLOSING
44 Notes
44 Final Thoughts
46 Maestro Memories
48 Resources

50 Appendix One
51 Appendix Two
52 Appendix Three

① INTRODUCTION

ABOUT THIS GUIDE

We hope you find this guidebook to be a useful resource for information and inspiration for Maestro Impro™.

This guide has been created to provide assistance for groups just starting out, clarity for those with questions, and a reminder for groups who have had some experience with the format to check in on their progress and development.

Here you will find information about the history of Maestro Impro™ and the spirit and theory behind the concept. We also provide practical information about the structure with a focus on skills and some tips on how to play the format as intended.

Most of the material in this study guide comes directly from Keith Johnstone himself, via his book IMPRO FOR STORYTELLERS and his 'Micetro Impro' 1990 and 'Gorilla and Micetro' November 1998 newsletters. The commentary and additional material is provided by improvisers from all over the world, many who have worked with Keith over the past 40 years, and official (or licensed) groups that perform Maestro Impro™ in the ITI community.

While this guide focuses on Maestro Impro™ - the format, we encourage you to build your improvisation skills in general through study with informed teachers. A list of suggested teachers can be found at: impro.global

Various resources are also located in a section at the end of this guide.

Enjoy your journey into the world of Maestro and may you find the fun, inspiration, and great potential for collaboration this format has to offer.

KEITH JOHNSTONE

by Doug Wong

Keith Johnstone was born in 1933 in Devon, England. He grew up hating school, finding that it blunted his imagination. His early tactic to combat the suppression of spontaneity and the creative mind was to enroll in teacher training college when he was refused entrance to University. Keith's success in applying his developing techniques in a Battersea Comprehensive with classes of children, categorized as 'average' and 'un-educatable' was undeniable.

The Divisional Officer of the school considered Keith 'not the right type' to enter the teaching profession and actively moved to end Keith's employment. Luckily, during a routine inspection by the education authority, the inspector who audited Keith's class was so impressed by his methods and the results he was achieving that the Divisional Officer was given firm instructions to allow him the freedom to continue developing his own pedagogy. Soon after, Keith wrote a list of 'things his teachers banned - like making faces' and used it as a syllabus.

In 1956 The Royal Court Theatre commissioned a play from him and he continued to work there until 1966, as unofficial head of the play-reading department, director and drama teacher, and eventually Associate Director.

In his early classes he began to question the impact schooling had on his imagination by exploring the reversal of what his teachers had taught him, in an attempt to create more spontaneous theatre actors. In Impro Keith writes, 'When I began teaching it was natural for me to reverse everything my own teachers had done. I got my actors to make faces, insult each other, always to leap before they looked, to scream and shout and misbehave in all sorts of ways'. It was at this time that Keith developed a series of improvisational exercises to help playwrights overcome writer's block and to assist actors in working more spontaneously.

He founded The Theatre Machine in the 1960s, an improvisation group which toured Europe and North America and was invited by the Canadian Government to perform at Expo 67. Keith moved to Calgary, Alberta, Canada in the 1970s, and in 1977 co-founded the Loose Moose Theatre Company.

Over the years, Keith created and evolved the globally recognized improvisation formats, Gorilla Theatre™, Maestro Impro™, Life Game and Theatresports™ which have gone on to be played in over 60 countries since the late 1970's.

Theatresports™ has become a staple of modern improvisational comedy and is the inspiration for television shows, 'Whose Line Is It Anyway?' (UK, USA), De Llamas, (NL) and Improv Heaven and Hell (Cdn) to name a few.

He is a Professor Emeritus of the University of Calgary and author of numerous essays, articles and productions which have been performed in Europe, North America, Africa and South America.

Most notably, Keith is known for his writing on Improvisation in the books IMPRO and IMPRO FOR STORYTELLERS translated to many languages and reaching the largest audiences of all his works in and outside the theatre communities and across cultures. (It was recently noted that his work outsold Stanislavsky in Germany.) Stanford University is home to The Keith Johnstone Papers which consist of original plays, writings, correspondence, theatrical materials, journals, artwork etc. Highlights of the collection include early chapter drafts of IMPRO and IMPRO FOR STORYTELLERS and some of Keith's original letters including letters to Keith from Del Close, Peter Coyote, Samuel Beckett, Harold Pinter, Anthony Stirling, Royal Court colleagues, Theatre Machine members etc.

THE INTERNATIONAL THEATRESPORTS™ INSTITUTE (ITI)

In 1998, the International Theatresports™ Institute (I.T.I.) was created to benefit the growing Improvisation community interested in Keith's work. It is the organization to which Keith Johnstone has entrusted the legacy of the format Theatresports™.

The ITI community is a Membership Association of groups and individuals joined together by a shared passion for the work of Keith Johnstone. Groups performing Johnstone's: Theatresports™, Maestro Impro™ and Gorilla Theatre™, apply for inexpensive performance rights. Schools are required to have performance rights as well for copyright reasons but there are no fees attached.

Members of this global community benefit from ongoing development and sharing of Keith Johnstone's work as well as the connection to each other. (Visit groups in Würzburg Germany or Calgary, Canada, and mention that you are the ITI member from Istanbul or Taipei and there will be a warm welcome and likely an invitation to join them on stage.)

Fees collected from performance rights go towards supporting its membership, passing on benefits and training to the community, as well as day to day management of the ITI. Benefits include Global seminars and gatherings every couple of years at the International ITI conferences held in various locations around the world.

Keith Johnstone has always refused to take any money from Theatresports™ royalties, allowing collected funds to be put back into community initiatives.

The ITI is here to support you and answer any questions you may have regarding Keith's work, including improvisation techniques, games, and the Maestro Impro™ format itself.

BEFORE PLAYING MAESTRO IMPRO™

As mentioned earlier, Maestro Impro™ is a copyright format, so before you begin, please contact the ITI and request the rights. The process is easy. Upon receiving the rights you become a member of the ITI community. This provides you with the format guide, Keith Johnstone newsletters, discounts to our conferences, and access to teachers, as well as connection to an international network of improvisers who are working with the same ideas and philosophy you are. It also shows a respect to the creative copyright of Keith Johnstone whose work you are exploring and who has enriched all of us, together in the improvisation community.

Please contact us at: admin@theatresports.org or visit: impro.global

MAESTRO IMPRO BACKGROUND

WHAT IS MAESTRO IMPRO™?

Maestro is an ensemble format featuring a large cast and directors. The show has an elimination structure where a mix of improvisers are randomly chosen to play scenes with each other. Two Directors set up the scenes and direct the players when needed. All scenes are scored by the audience based on how much they enjoyed it.

The players given the highest scores continue while those with lower scores leave the show, eliminated after each round until only one improviser remains. This player is The Maestro.

On one level Maestro might be viewed by the audience as competition between players, with arbitrary combinations of performers of varying skills peppered with seemingly unfair eliminations. The show, however, is a well crafted structure that ultimately protects the audience by giving them an effective show arc, consistently retaining the most inspired performers until the end of the show. The performers understand that Maestro is most effectively played with benevolence and good nature towards the other players, with the ultimate goal of creating an enjoyable evening for the audience leaving them with memories of engaging scenes full of variety. Improvisers are admired for working together to create inspiring scenes despite having different levels of experience and skill.

The Big If - Impro Festival Barcelona, Spain
by Riccardo Salamanna

MAESTRO ORIGINS

Maestro was born out of necessity. Keith invented Maestro in Utrecht, The Netherlands after working with some students in an Impro class. At the end of the workshop, he needed a format that could include many students of differing abilities. Under Keith's direction, Maestro sprang into existence that night and the problem was solved. The format was further developed in Calgary at The Loose Moose Theatre during some Thursday night show experiments into a format where each element was tempered to serve a purpose and where it has been played since 1995. The experiment proved itself and Maestro is now found on stages from Oslo to Tokyo in festivals and as the mainstay of improvisation companies.

THE NAME

There is confusion in some circles over the spelling of Maestro. Whereas some groups use M-a-e-s-t-r-o, others are still following the outdated spelling M-i-c-e-t-r-o. In IMPRO FOR STORYTELLERS Keith Johnstone refers to the format as 'Micetro'. His original idea was to compare the game to mice running a race through a labyrinth. He liked the comparison of the mice learning as time goes on, to how improviser progress and how the show improves as it progresses. The pun overlaps with the word 'Maestro' - referring to the master of the show - Number 1 in the race to be the best.

Over the years, however, Keith himself recognized the Micetro idea was a little confusing and didn't work as a title in some countries where the word-play simply doesn't make sense. As of 2014, Keith has officially asked groups to use the simpler spelling of Maestro.

Impro Melbourne
Melbourne, Australia
📷 by Impro Melbourne

MAESTRO AROUND THE WORLD

As of this writing, Maestro is played in over 20 countries. It has quickly become a favourite format to perform during international festivals as it can incorporate many people during opening and closing presentations. It has also become a useful tool in cities hoping to bring diverse groups and individuals together on stage and as a way of developing a stronger Impro culture.

Styles vary slightly from company to company but generally, Maestro maintains greater cohesiveness than most formats have over the years. This has allowed for easy integration of guests from outside the community. The broad possibilities within the format increase access to those with varied improvisation backgrounds. (There is something to be said for joyful interaction on the same stage between the sometimes distant schools of improvisers.)

Companies playing Maestro around the world can be reached through the ITI.

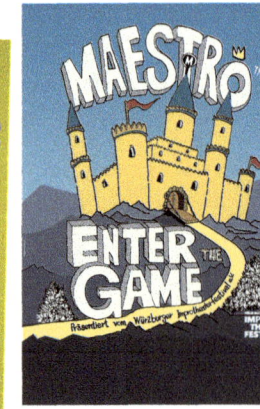

Design by Daniel Orrantia

> » Maestro is the perfect format for us to have international improvisers as guest players. The audience enjoys watching unbelievable collaboration as if we could talk in the same language. «
>
> *Takayuki Ueda · IMPACT360, Osaka, Japan*

WHAT MAESTRO CAN ACHIEVE

Maestro has qualities which can benefit the groups playing it while, at the same time, entertaining audiences. Knowing what your group or company wants and needs is an integral part of artistic direction.

If played with the intended integrity, Maestro can achieve:

- Integration of large numbers of performers into a cohesive performance
- Development of a group with varied experience and expertise
- Improvement of and proficiency in directing skills
- A relatively easy introduction to improvisation for newer or less skilled players
- Leadership capacity for advanced players
- Continued benefits in formatting an arc of performance that get stronger through the evening rather than performing shows that consistently have no shape or worse, consistently start high and end low
- Groups performing Maestro on a regular basis develop a loyal audience base, excited to come back to watch players compete each week and cheer on their favourites

Picnic Improvisación Teatral
Monkey Fest
Bogota, Colombia
📷 *by Fernanda Pineda*

I Bugiardini
Rome, Italy
📷 *by Elisa Pizza*

3 IMPORTANT CONCEPTS

HOW MAESTRO IS UNIQUE

Maestro embodies the general concepts of Improvisation understood by most improvisers. The format itself however, stands out with such elements as:
· A high quality show that embraces a mixed level of performers
· Directors who help add variation to the performance
· A seemingly incongruous element of competitive elimination in a typically supportive improvisation arena

Aside from its proven worth as a performance, Maestro proves itself as an exceptional teaching tool for groups. Maestro is a way for experienced players and new players to interact and learn from each other. As easy as it would be to say that Maestro allows new players to learn from experienced players, it has an equally strong impact on seasoned performers. More skilled players can view improvisation with a fresh perspective by working with players who are newer to the stage and with whom they may not otherwise play. In larger communities of disconnected companies, Maestro has had a positive impact of integrating varied groups and individual improvisers together with a strong spirit of community.

Within the show, there are many skills being trained. Whether the desire is to improve the overview of the Director's eye and spontaneous devising skills, or in working on evolving stage skills, Maestro helps. If companies have a desire to engage audiences with a selfless style of improvisation that gives the audience a feeling of control, Maestro is a good choice.

> » I love how supportive the format is; we use Maestro as an opportunity to mix up the tiers of our company and get them playing together. We also have an audience volunteer play in the show too! «
> *Matt Schuurman - Rapid Fire Theatre, Edmonton, Canada*

THE SPIRIT

Keith's formats and style are unique in the improvisation community. Understanding the foundation of Keith's work with regards to the spirit and intent will aid in the playing of Maestro and improvisation in general.

Aspects of The Spirit include:
· Playfulness
· Supporting your partner and valuing their ideas
· Risk taking
· Honesty and vulnerability
· Being positive
· Failure - Learning to fail gracefully and good-naturedly
· Teamwork
· Misbehavior

The format always shows what is most important, not skill but helping each other and enjoying the moment together.

RISK AND FAILURE

Risk, for many of us, is a stepping stone towards embarrassing failure. It is normal to protect ourselves from judgment and stress. Protecting ourselves from failure is common in everyday life but that same self-protection used on stage leads to self-censorship and the removal of risk. We minimize the chance of failure by making weak choices or taking no risks at all.

In order to take risks we need to embrace a perspective that failure is our partner and not the enemy. With this relationship in mind, improvisers can play freely and fearlessly.

The structure of Maestro has some safety built in which encourages risk taking but performers and Directors must still be reminded to take a risk. Through the Directors, Maestro players are given greater license to make choices which they might normally shy away from. The Director will help get them back on track if the scene is struggling. Be careful however, not to adopt a view of failure where the group seeks to create artificial mistakes. When performers see the idea of failure as valuable in and of itself, they may play stupidly or pretend to make mistakes. This looks (and feels) contrived and forced. Play to your highest intelligence. Failure will happen without trying to make it appear.

Picnic Improvisación Teatral - Monkey Fest
Bogota, Colombia
by Sebastián Gomez

TEAMWORK

Maestro IS teamwork. The show can be packaged as a competitive struggle, survival of the fittest, a cage match ending with one person left standing (which is how many groups advertise it), but the deeper story is that Maestro's performers, Directors, technicians, volunteers and audience are all on the same team.

Maestro builds layers of support. The eyes of the Director are there to benefit what the onstage performer might be missing. The offstage performers are there to support a scene that the Director may have lost connection with. And the audience is there at the end to reaffirm what they want and correct the outcome with their votes. Maestro isn't about individual glory, but a focus on working collectively to give the audience a good show. The audience returns week after week as part of that team.

I Bugiardini - Rome, Italy
by Elisa Pizza

SKILLS

The structure of a well constructed format offers added insurance, which can care for the improvisers and audience on nights when the performers might not be at their peak. However, reliance on format alone is no replacement for development of skills. Skill building will help you to create the content to fill the frame of the Maestro format.

Here are some more Impro fundamentals followed by related games/exercises from IMPRO FOR STORYTELLERS:

The Big If - Impro Festival, Barcelona, Spain
by Riccardo Salamanna

Spontaneity/Present Moment

Our fear of being judged and our desire to be liked keeps us searching in our heads for what to do next. As improvisers we train how to be present; otherwise we don't see or hear what's happening, can't react honestly and won't be able to work effectively with our partners.

These are some living in the now training scenes/exercises:

- Wide Eyes – pg. 205/206
- Emotional Sounds – pg. 268-270
- Emotional Goals – pg. 184/185
- Hat Games – pg. 19, 156-161
- Mantras – pg. 270-274
- Sandwiches – pg. 236/237
- Making Faces – pg. 162-168

Control

Control issues come into focus from two sides: Those who will never give up control and those who never take control or make offers.

For those who will not relinquish control, this behaviour (connected to fear) keeps us from accepting our partner's offers. It keeps us in the unchanging emotional state we have chosen to hang on to. It keeps us safe, we reveal nothing about ourselves and go scene after scene without being altered in any way.

Conversely, the fear of taking control puts all the pressure on our partners to make offers and move the scene forward. The fear of getting it wrong screams at us, "Follow! Don't do anything except what is asked of you!"

In Maestro there can be an issue with players who have trained out their ability to take initiative. They get used to listening to Directors and don't develop their own skills of making strong offers and launching their own scenes. Other players may resent an outside voice or perspective and want to ignore good advice. Or they may not want to play a secondary, passenger role in an entire scene when that is exactly what is needed. In Maestro, finding a balance between the two sides of control is a worthwhile goal. Here are some exercises that play with shared or shifting responsibility:

- Tug of War pg. 57/58
- Word at a Time – pg. 114-115, 131-134, 329
- One Voice – pg. 171-177
- He said/she said (Stage Directions) – pg. 195-199
- Dubbing (Synchro) – pg. 171 -178
- Moving Bodies – pg. 200-202
- Passengers - pg. 230

Being Physical

Security agents at an airport listen to how much you talk when they ask you questions. Stressed people speak a lot and keep talking long after what was asked has been answered. This state can be seen everywhere stress is in play. Talking too much and explaining away our feelings and desires is a primary human defence. For the improviser, an alternative is to play physically so the body can tell the stories instead of the intellect. Trusting the body takes the pressure off the mind to do all the work.

Players and Directors should notice when the show is getting stiff and verbal. They should be on the lookout for ways to add physicality even with side characters or scenic elements. Physical group scenes are possible especially in the first rounds.

Here are some exercises to focus on the physical side.
· Justify the Gesture – pg. 193-195
· Gibberish – pg. 185/186, 214-219
· Changing the Body Image – pg. 276-277
· People as Objects – pg. 303-304
· Sit/Stand/lie – pg. 366/367

Status

Status exists in every moment. It creates a direct line towards defining relationship between characters and between the environment and the characters. It is our relative importance to everything and everyone around us. Our status is a part of our personae that is in constant movement in relationship to the world we exist in. Playing with status elements reveals dramatic and fascinating human behaviour which the audience relates to on a deep level.

Here are some exercises that look at status interaction.
· Various Status Exercises – pg. 219-231
· Master/Servant – pg. 240/241
· Making Faces – pg. 162-168
· Pecking Orders – pg. 168
· King Game – pg. 237-240

Narrative

An audience sees story in everything and will remember the stories in the improvisation long after the games and gags are forgotten. We recommend fostering storytelling skills. They provide the tools needed to create an evening of interesting improvised theatre and not just hours of filler and fluff. Using these skills, performers become less reliant on games, quick jokes and gags.

If we can learn to see and react to hints of story, we gain insight into what might come next. The turn of a shoulder makes the story about seduction. The glare of the boss' eyes make the story shift from a firing to something more sinister. Every offer is a promise that the audience reads something into. Understanding the natural tendency to see the story in all that we do should compel us to nurture and develop effective narrative skills.

Aside from using structured narrative exercises like the ones listed below, Maestro Directors look for opportunities to guide the narrative in open scenes and even to pull story structure out of games. Interrogations for example should not just be guessing games but a piecing together of the story puzzle.
· Various Story Games – pg. 130-154
· What Comes Next – pg. 134-142
· Typing Game – pg. 151-154
· Word at a Time – pg. 114-115, 131-134, 329

A dangerous pitfall for improvisers is behaviour that enables them to avoid the unknown. Making needless jokes at the expense of the story, remaining distant and unaffected and wimping or not defining what must be defined are all destructive tactics. Directors and teachers need to be aware of these evasions and encourage players to fearlessly continue.

>> We discovered that a good Maestro should always have one or two people on stage with no or very very little experience. That for us just always makes better shows. <<
Gerald Weber - Theatre Anundpfirsich, Zurich, Switzerland

PREPARATION

WHAT YOU NEED FOR MAESTRO

- 1 or 2 Directors
- 12-15 Improvisers (in a 90 min to 2 hour show. 9-12 improvisers in a 60 minute show)
- 1 Emcee whose primary job is to take scores from the audience between scenes
- Clipboard/pen/paper for Emcee to take scene notes
- 1 Scorekeeper whose purpose is to keep the scores up to date on a visible board
- Clipboard/pen/paper for Scorekeeper to take scoring/ player notes
- 1 Scoreboard large enough for audience to clearly see the progression of players
- 12-15 Name cards - (if your scoreboard can slide names along)
- Pens/chalk/stickynotes/etc. - Depending what your scoring system requires
- 12-15 Numbered pinnies or buttons with securing mechanism (clips/pins/magnets)
- 12-15 Numbered coins - To be drawn from bowl by Directors
- 2 Bowls - one to take numbers from and one to drop them in
- 1 Prize
- 1 Audience
- Extra - Scenographers, props, costumes, technicians, musicians, lights, sound

The Scoreboard

Groups around the world have tried various structures to maintain and present the ongoing scoring in a Maestro show. Typical presentations include sliding cards with the performer's name written on them. The name plates move down numbered tracks like racehorses advancing along a two-dimensional course - which the Norwegian improvisers in Oslo have crafted - albeit with a range of other animals riding down the rails. The name plates on the board corresponds to the numbers that players onstage wear on their clothing. (See photo on pg. 53)

Other groups use chalk on chalkboards or markers on whiteboards with numbers refreshed as scoring goes on through the night. Some Impro groups, in recent years have incorporated projected scoreboards that are dimmed between scenes and shine away from the main performance space. (You might be able to contact one of these companies to purchase the apps they have designed for their projected scoreboards). One German group used giant lego towers stacked up for each player as they accumulated points.

The scoreboard should be raised and in a position that is accessible to the Scorekeeper but also visible to the Directors and audience. Names and numbers should be clearly written so they can be read from a distance.

》 People should not 'leap in'. Start by playing a twenty minute game with less players. When you are skilled, play the professional game. 《
Keith Johnstone

Der Kaktus - Würzburg, Germany
 *by Nicolas Dreher*

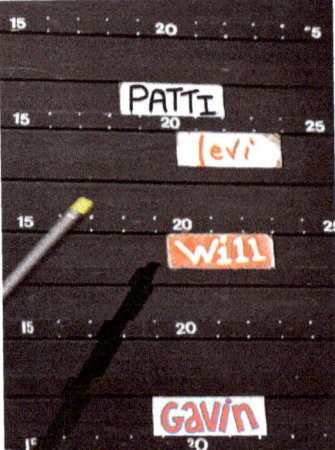

Loose Moose Theatre - Calgary, Canada
by Kate Ware

Pinnies/Buttons

In Maestro, each player wears a visible number that the Directors and audience can clearly see. Those numbers relate to the numbered coins in the bowls and player scores on the board. A light sports vest (pinnie) with the number printed on the front makes it the most visible but big buttons, stickers or arm bands also work. It is important that the numbers are well connected to their wearer and don't go flying off in physical scenes. If you use buttons, pins are possible but magnets are safer.

Coins/Bowls

In front of the Directors are two shallow bowls. One holds the numbers which correspond to the number of players in the cast. The other one is the discard bowl. At the Loose Moose theatre in Calgary the discard bowl is metallic. The numbers are written on both sides of big metal coins and create a satisfying, substantial sound as the coin is discarded into the metal bowl. It helps if the bowls look different. Keeping the two bowls defined helps avoid confusion about which bowl to draw the next players from. Having the numbers printed in big, bold font on both sides of the coins helps for making quick and easy identification in the low light condition of the theatre.

Many companies use ping pong balls with numbers. After a couple of mistaken fumbles where the balls end up rolling across the stage, you'll understand why the large coins are preferable.

Loose Moose Theatre Calgary, Canada
by Heather Smith

Duration

Typically Maestro is played as a two-hour show including a fifteen minute interval after the first hour. (The second half should be a little shorter than the first half.)
Some groups who are limited with time, perform with a smaller cast in shows ranging from 45-75 minutes without a break.

The Space

For years, Maestro played at the Cairo Kultur House in Würzburg, Germany took place in a tiny room, crowded with less than 25 audience members while the Maestro cast of 12 was crammed into window ledges and on the edge of the stage when they weren't performing. These evenings were fun and full of energy. Eventually their success forced the show upstairs to a more typical arrangement for Maestro in a larger venue.

The preferable space for Maestro is a stage that can accommodate the entire cast, sitting on the edge of or just off the stage without too much crowding. It's nice to have seating on either side of the stage so that all players have easy access if they are called up or are inspired to enter into someone else's scene.

Be cautious about placing offstage improvisers too close to the lit areas of the performance space as they can become unwanted distractions to the work on stage.

Another reason not to have players visible for the whole show is that it relieves them from being 'on' all the time. It is easier to support the show in a relaxed way without constant performance pressure.

Placement of Directors

Typically the two Maestro Directors sit where they have the best view of the performers on stage. Don't shy away from placing the Directors front row centre. It can give the show a sense of breaking the invisible wall, which highlights a difference between traditional theatre and improvisation. This also allows for the best directing vantage point. Groups like Det Andre Teatret and Loose Moose Theatre leave a middle seat between the two Directors. This is functional as it gives access to the bowls of numbers corresponding to players, hats (for hat games) and whatever else the Directors wish to have handy. Groups like Impro Melbourne will place a small table in front of Directors to hold the Director's accessories. Additionally in some spaces, a microphone (on a stand or lapel mics) are used to amplify the Director's voices so that even people in the back of the theatre can hear what is being said. If directing with your back to the audience, speak loud so that everyone can hear.

Impro Melbourne - Melbourne, Australia
by Mark Gambino

BEFORE THE SHOW

Theatre Anundpfirsich - Zurich, Switzerland
by Theatre Anundpfirsich

Warm-up Class

In numerous improvisation theatres playing Maestro, a pre-show class engages the company in a practical warm up for the evening show. It's possible to consider the weakness of the previous show and touch upon the skills that might need to be worked on. If the last show lacked characters being altered, for example, you could work on that element in the pre-show class of the upcoming show. The warm-up class is useful for the Directors as well because it allows them to see who is available and who might be in a good state for that night's performance. This arrangement isn't a perfect indicator of the state of the performers, but it does help in a situation where the Directors may have never met some of the players they will be working with.

Be careful not to set the class up like an audition for the show. The aim is to reduce the pressure and get people to interact in a healthy way. We don't want them competing for spots. Some groups make the pre-show class mandatory and some leave it open for whomever would like to participate regardless of their role in the show.

Some groups pre-cast their shows in advance but still leave the class open to the entire company.

The warm up class offers a positive benefit socially as well as development of Impro skills.

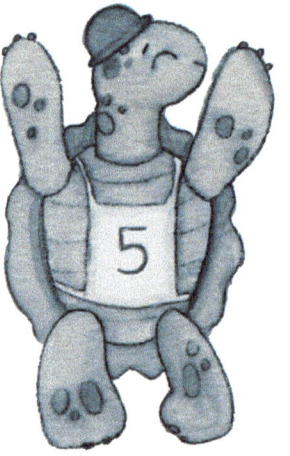

>> A game that opens with three excellent scenes is in serious trouble because it leaves you nowhere to go except down. (Jack Benny said the same thing about getting a standing ovation when he stepped on stage). We don't need wonderful scenes at the start, and a disastrous scene can be very valuable in making the audience understand that improvisation is not as easy as it sometimes looks! <<
Keith Johnstone

Pre-Show Meeting

The pre-show meeting following the class is essential to the running of the show. This ritual of gathering together and going over the roles has a unifying and focussing effect.

Some groups choose players before the meeting but many will select performers just before the show. A cast of 12-15 performers will be selected from those attending the meeting.

Those running the pre show meeting: assign roles, remind company members of what they might try to achieve, and any other notes that will aid in a positive experience for the audience.

In some theatres, the Director or the Directors are the ones running the pre-show meeting, while in others, pre-determined individuals are in charge. Regardless of who runs the meeting, there should be an efficiency and attention to the needs of the company and performance.

Be sure that the technical crew is ready. It is good to pre-select the technical improvisers who might need time to prepare sound, have requirements for instruments where live music is incorporated, or acclimate themselves to the light board etc. This is a good time to introduce these technical improvisers by name and point out any technical elements that might concern the rest of the cast. (eg: The stage will be mopped before the show, so walk carefully, the lights on stage left have been giving us some issues so prepare to move if the lights suddenly disappear….etc.)

Some groups choose the Emcee before the evening meeting but in a theatre group where there is confidence that the role can be filled during the pre-show meeting, then there is a pleasant element that the person who is volunteering for the role is doing it because they are inspired at that moment.

The group is asked, "who would like to play?". If more hands go up than can be accommodated on stage, the person in charge picks the appropriate number to play. They choose participants based on various qualities partly determined by the values of what your company is trying to achieve. While it might seem that skill level is the most important thing to choose performers for, consider that in some theatres Maestro is being used as a training format to encourage new players to wet their feet and develop their skills. Who you choose is up to you. We suggest a mix of performers from relatively experienced people to newer improvisers.

Impro Japan
Tokyo, Japan
📷 by Impro Japan

With the large cast of Maestro, scenographers can be the offstage players who help move set pieces or clear away props and objects off stage after scenes. Alternatively, dedicated scenographers who are not players can be chosen at the discretion of the show Director.

The needs in your theatre will dictate other roles that may not have been mentioned here. The pre-show meeting is a good time to organize the company into positions that will ensure that your evening runs smoothly. (Who sets up the chairs? Who is in charge after the show to make sure everyone puts away costumes and props? Who is in charge of telling the technicians when all the player are in place for the show opening etc.) Some groups designate a Stage Manager who is responsible for doing or delegating these jobs. Having a stage manager also takes the burden off the Directors who are thinking about the upcoming show and might rather have someone deflect pre-show questions or concerns.

MAESTRO IN DETAIL

THE START OF THE SHOW

*Rapid Fire Theatre
Edmonton, Canada
by Marc Julien Objois*

The Emcee:
· welcomes the audience
· introduces the group/company, the show, themself and the Directors
· explains how the audience will award points after each scene and rehearses the the vote

They invite the players on stage, who introduce themselves efficiently by saying their name. If your cast has visiting guests, those players might say where they are from. Some groups find it is nice to introduce where you are from even if it is local suburb, but when extra information is added at the top of the show, it should be done with efficiency and not as an habitual rule or behaviour. If the Maestro from the previous show is there, they can be introduced as last week/month's winner. Then we see the prize and finally the focus is passed on to the Directors.

SAMPLE OPENING

· "Welcome to Keith Johnstone's Maestro Impro™.
· Tonight we feature 13 players who will perform scenes led by our two Directors. (names)
· The Directors will draw coins from a bowl with numbers on them. The numbers correspond to the numbers each player wears and to the ones we see up on the scoreboard.
· You, the audience, will score the scenes and throughout the evening, based on their scores, players will be eliminated. By the end of the night, only one improviser will remain and they become tonight's Maestro."
(Voting rehearsal as below)

· Now let's meet tonight's players.
(The players enter, line up on stage and introduce themselves.)
Note: This is not rigid formality. They don't have to enter in order like school children lined up in the correct numerical order.
And our improvisers will be playing for the coveted Five Dollar Bill (the prize for the winner)
(Show the prize.)
Now I'll pass the focus over to our Directors.
Enjoy the show!"

» I've always called the host the 'scorekeeper' because I don't want them to take over and start entertaining the audience. Calling them the host gives them too much power. «   *Keith Johnstone*

The primary function of this role is to take the vote for points and give the audience the information they need at the top of the show. With the help of the Scorekeeper, the Emcee facilitates the running of the show, keeping the scores up to date and making a scene list which can aid in the note session after the show.
While the Emcee is responsible for taking votes, closing the show is typically left to the winning player of Maestro.

THE EMCEE AND SCOREKEEPER

The Emcee makes announcements and advertises other shows at the top of second half, including introducing the technical improvisers and support staff to the audience, (backstage scenographers, lights, sound, volunteers, etc.)
In general the Emcee should be efficient, charming and able to control the audience effectively when needed.
They should not aim to be funny or entertaining. Their job is to make the format clear and help the show run efficiently. They are not a coach, nor a judge, and must be careful not to put their opinion into the process of scene judgement - leave that to the audience.

> *A good Emcee can keep things moving along and won't hog the limelight.* «
> *Tom Salinsky - The Spontaneity Shop, London, England*

VOTING/SCORING

The vote description at the beginning of the show should use simple terminology. "1 is for a scene you didn't like and 5 is for a scene you really liked." The tendency for almost all Emcees is to say "1 is for a horrible, rotten, terrible scene and 5 is for the best, greatest thing ever!" Expressing the range in this way makes it difficult for the audience to vote for 1's and 5's and leads to issues when eliminations must be made.

Practice the voting procedure. This practice trains the audience to express themselves and encourages permission to vote the full range of scores.

First, have them practice a low vote. Suggest they have just watched a scene they didn't like. Count through the score and make sure they understand that was the time for them to vote for 1's and 2's. Follow that with a practice vote for a scene they liked. If they understood your instructions, they should now be applauding for 4's and 5's. It is typical with repeat audiences that they will misbehave and some people will purposefully vote contrary to what you want them to during the practice round. Make sure that audience voting during the practice vote is clearly understood otherwise there will be problems later in the show.

By ending with the positive vote we hope to move to the next section of the show with a positive feeling.

This little script succinctly explains the practice vote:

"After each scene you will give it a score based on a scale of 1-5. Let's say you saw a scene that you did not enjoy. Was that a 1 (emphasis), a 2 - 3 - 4 - 5? (going faster through the latter numbers to dissuade audience members who just want to make jokes.) Now let's say you saw a scene you enjoyed. Was that a 1 - 2 - 3 - 4 (briskly through the first few numbers) or a 5? (emphasis)."

Note: The emphasis is only to help illustrate the voting procedure. Be cautious never to emphasize any particular number in regular scoring.

Picnic Improvisación Teatral - Monkey Fest Bogota, Colombia by Fernanda Pineda

Det Andre Teatret - Oslo, Norway by Kjetil Aavik

> *The practice vote allows the audience to give fives and ones.* «
> *Keith Johnstone*

During the show, when scenes end, performers leave the stage and sit at the side. The Emcee comes on to take the vote. As mentioned earlier, vocal inflection when saying the numbers to the audience should be the same for each so as not to influence their vote. Based on volume and enthusiasm of the audience's vote, the Emcee declares the score. For example, "That scene was worth a 3." The show continues while the scorekeeper quietly updates the scores for the players involved in the scene.

If the applause for two numbers sounds similar and the Emcee is unsure which one most of the audience is clapping for, the Emcee should be encouraged to take the lower number. Where they heard identical scoring for 3 and 2, they can simply announce, "That scene was worth a 2."

Choosing the lower score has significance because we never want to seem better than we are. If the audience is unhappy with the choice, they are likely to be louder when they vote next time. If they voice disapproval, they can be encouraged to fight more for the number they want next time.

Overall, we are trying to convince the audience that we take their votes seriously. So we occasionally re-vote when the scoring is too close to call. When the vote is split - applause for 4 and 5 are similar for example. - the audience is told, there will be a vote for just those two numbers. "Was that a 4?" (wait for applause) "Was that a 5?" (wait for applause) At that point a decision is made. Even a wrong decision is better than delaying the show further. This is a tool to use sparingly, but it can be fun to hear the audience re-vote more emphatically to get their opinion across.

*I Bugiardini
Rome, Italy
by Elisa Piz...*

Maestro Emcees can support audience members who are in the minority and have scored low. If a woman is quietly clapping for a score of 1 all by herself, she will become quiet almost instantly when she hears that no one is supporting her opinion. The Emcee may say, "Yes! Vote what you believe!". That subtle encouragement might embolden others who were too shy to vote low when that is what they actually thought of the scene.

We aren't trying to get the audience to vote low. We are trying to get the audience to express themselves honestly because most theatres in the world imply their work is above the audience, and if it's not appreciated, it is the audience's fault, not the performers, Directors and writers. In Improvisation, that could couldn't be further from our intentions.

If necessary, remind the audience that only applause will be counted, not cheering.

If people cheer, explain that it is easy to judge the audience's opinion of a scene by their applause but cheering makes it impossible to judge fairly. Loud voices or hooting and hollering can disrupt the outcome of the show leaving a final group of players that the majority of the audience didn't choose.

It is a good idea for the Scorekeeper to write down the number of each player in the current scene as they are chosen by the Director. This helps to keep track of which name cards will be moved ahead after the vote.

Note: Sometimes we remind the audience that their vote decides the winner of the show, we do this if every score is the same and to remind them of the value of the vote and that they are shaping the show ahead.

> » We have promised a reward for the first players that will achieve 1 for their scenes. We still did not have one. It happens not because we are such good players but because the audience is still too polite!«
> *Giuseppe Marchei, i Bugiardini, Rome, Italy*

SCENE ROUNDS

Typically in a show where 12 or 13 performers appear, early rounds tend to have more people and more structure. While this is typical, it is not a rule. A two person scene after a four person game adds to the variety.
An example of rounds might look like this:
- Round one: a mix of 2, 3 and 4 person scenes (no elimination). It is likely that there will be more games or structures in these rounds.
- Round two: a mix of 2, 3, 4 person scenes, possibly ending with our first solo of the night.
- First elimination. Typically the first half has lasted approximately 50 minutes. (interval, if need be)
- Lightning Round (a speed Round facilitating a quicker tempo and scoring diversity - see below): for variety and to get to the next elimination more quickly.
- Last two or three rounds: longer scenes, two person scenes, unless there's a good reason to add a third person. More solos. (typically less game structures)
- Tie Breaker or Showdown to end the night unless one player is far ahead.

As the structure of Maestro dictates, scene rounds become shorter as eliminations are made and fewer players are left. This is intentional and adds to an increasing intensity which develops the proper show arc.

LIGHTNING ROUNDS

Consider a situation where you have finished a round of scenes and are ready to eliminate players. Unfortunately, you look at the scoreboard and recognize that too many or too few players would be eliminated. One option is that you play a quick Lightning Round. A Lightning round is a series of one minute scenes which typically impose variety in the scoring, making it easier to eliminate by shaking up the scores a little.

It should be understood that these scenes last a maximum of one minute but can certainly be shorter. If the feeling is to bring the lights down after 30 seconds, by all means do so.

Generally, after two rounds and the first elimination, if there are still many performers in the game or if the remaining improvisers all have similar scores, it is a good time for this procedure.

In a lightning round, Directors should give little or no direction. One round devoid of initial suggestions can encourage players to initiate. With time pressure, action tends to move forward quicker and the subconscious can be tricked into opening up. Scenes are often lighter and less precious.

Beyond being an elimination tool, lightning rounds can also spice up the show in tempo and attitude but they are not a must. Putting Lightning rounds in as regular procedure is not recommended.

>> We are improvisors putting on a play about competing in a show. The drama is in the tension of the eliminations. So enjoy them! <<
Jeff Gladstone - Vancouver, Canada

Det Andre Teatret
Oslo, Norway
Kjetil Aavik

ELIMINATIONS

A round ends when all remaining players have been awarded points for being in a scene. There is usually no elimination after the first round so that each player can have at least two scenes. Eliminations should occur after round two. The number of players to eliminate is the Director's choice.

Eliminating too many, too early could be disastrous if you leave too few players to fill the rest of the allotted time. Not eliminating enough performers defeats the strength of Maestro to create a flow towards more consistently strong scenes as your pool of players is thinned to the evening's strongest participants.

When Directors call the names of those to be eliminated, players should step forward and wave goodbye to the audience. It should be clear who is out of the game and who will continue. Players leave humbly and happy about the part they played.

They hang their pinnies on the side or drop their number tags into a box.

Elimination in Maestro means players are out of the the game. They find a place to watch the rest of the show. If there are roles to support the show that haven't been filled like providing scenography, counting the scores or taking scene notes and statistics, they can move into that function. Don't invite eliminated players to enter scenes. Part of the Maestro training is for players at all levels to practice support of those who are still in the game. We trust that the Directors and remaining performers will handle the rest of the show as the cast dwindles down to the final survivor. Jumping into scenes once players are eliminated diffuses the potential drama of the eliminations.

DIRECTORS

Who Should Direct

Directing is a skill to be fostered. Directing improvisation is a different beast than traditional theatre directing. Ideally, Maestro Directors are experienced players who have spent time teaching, coaching or leading Impro groups. Directors of Impro should be able to keep their wits about them while under pressure and keep their egos in check. The best Directors are often those who know innately how to inspire their partners, can react confidently and understand the needs of the show. They have strong storytelling skills, and understand a range of game structures.

» Good and selfless Directors are needed and are hard to come by. «
Tom Salinsky - The Spontaneity Shop, London, England

Responsibility

The Directors are viewed by the audience as ultimately responsible for the quality of the scenes. Having skilled Directors can help free players of the pressure to be perfect, relevant or funny, however we must train performers to take initiative to make the Director irrelevant. With a good Director, the players can be emboldened to explore truth and to improvise with commitment.

The whole ensemble, including players in technical roles, work as a team to create a show full of risk and variety. Here is how Keith describes framing the Director's role:

Picnic Improvisación Teatral - Monkey Fest Bogota, Colombia
by Fernanda Pineda

》 The Directors are responsible for the success of the game. This should be explained by the Emcee at the start of the show, and can - and perhaps should - be repeated after any scene that receives a very low score: And the Directors were responsible for the quality of that scene. 《

Keith Johnstone

Challenges

Directing Maestro can be challenging, rewarding, overwhelming and a practice in staying calm while the show whips around you like a tornado.

In a normal scenario, you are sitting beside another Director for two hours of Impro, setting up scenes and trying to help the improvisers create a varied evening of entertainment with a wide range of stories, some interesting images, some bits of craziness and dealing calmly with the occasional improvisational shipwreck. Some scenes are directed with an idea initially in the mind of the Director. ('Romance at the office of a politician') Most are directed as response to the needs of the performers. (The two improvisers I picked are staring each other like… spies. It's a spy scene.)

The best way to learn to get it right is to start doing it and make mistakes. Since you are improvising too, don't expect to do a perfect job.

- The ongoing challenge is to speak relevant information at the right time.
- The other challenge is to keep your mouth shut when the performers are making the relevant choices.

》 I think my first experience as a director in Maestro Impro™ was one of the more stressful I had on stage. Now, just 8 years later :-), I am little bit more relaxed when I play Maestro Impro™ as a Director. 《

Giuseppe Marchei - i Bugiardini, Rome, Italy

Coup de Comedy Festival Orange County, USA
by Dale Dudeck

>> You don't have to try and save every scene. <<
Keith Johnstone

*Det Andre Teatret
Oslo, Norway
by Kjetil Aavik*

Who and When to Direct

In a typical Maestro evening you might have 12 improvisers to draw from. 3 of them might be your top improvisers who do shows with consistent success. 3 of them might be new to your company and tonight is the very first time they've stepped on stage. The other 6 smiling individuals are improvisers with experience somewhere in between the other two groups. With the random selection of performers in the first rounds of the show you are certain to have a mix of skills represented which will call for your full attention.

After some eliminations you will hopefully find yourself with your strongest players chosen by the audience. At this point, your directing can be more measured in terms of suggestions. Trust the performers who have lasted through rounds of elimination. It should feel like freeing the reins and letting the horses run as the show moves forward.

You are not a rigid full-time Director in a strict sense, instead, a flexible Director who knows when to give up control as the show requires. By design, a Maestro Director's biggest challenge comes at the start of the night and lessens as the eliminations cut away those who might have needed your help more.

Preparation for Directing

Before the show, some Directors create a list of reminders with a variety of ideas about aspects of the show:
- scene inspirations (scene in a space station, Jack and the Beanstalk from the giant's point of view, a gardner making contact with the rabbit who steals his carrots)
- characters (the last polar bear, a humanoid alien encountering humanity, a racist grandparent)
- actor-direction (asking a question like what's your new year's resolution? What element of society pisses you off? What did you want to be as a child?)
- elements that add variety (Dear Diary game for a solo scene, scene in another language, radio play in the dark)

You might want to consider reminders that include numbers of people (a few solo scene possibilities, a few 4 person exercises etc.)

Use this sort of cheat sheet resource only when needed. Over-planning is a risk because it might blind you to what is actually occuring in the moment on stage in favour of pre-planned thoughts that aren't relevant to the moment.

Follow your own instincts and those of the improvisers. Your lists are suggestions for a hypothetical show. The actual show on stage often calls for something different than anything you could possibly plan. Good directors might create notes before the show and look back at the end of the evening to see they did almost nothing on their list. For many people, this sort of list can bolster the confidence of the director as a way to say, if all things fail, here's a possibility or two. With the extra confidence, most directors won't need the list at all because their spontaneous mind feels safe enough to react.

*Loose Moose Theatre
Calgary, Canada*
📷 *by Heather Smith*

Choosing the Players
(see Coins/Bowls section above)
90% of the time Directors are randomly picking numbers from the bowls. But on occasion they might want to choose specific players for specific reasons. For example:
- a performer who is comfortable with a solo scene
- putting a guest in the show with a player who will take care of them
- developing a player's skills and partnering them with certain others who might help
- trying a mask or music scene in that part of the show with a person who is inspired by the idea
- when many have the same score, choosing the players with different scores from each other - for more score diversity

The bowls should be wide and shallow. Why? Because it makes it easier to see the numbers when creative manipulation of player choice comes in handy. Directors shouldn't abuse the ability to manipulate the numbers but need not become too rigid about following the rule that choices are 100% random. If a choice helps inspire the cast, creates a better show, develops the performers or leaves the audience happier than when they came in, then it's possible to bend the rules in aid of the show. (Use that suggestion sparingly!) There are some groups that go out of their way to prove that the numbers are randomly chosen. They have the Emcee pick the number or have the other Director pick them.

But saying, "Shawn, pick three numbers for me" is a rather inefficient way to get people on stage when you could simply take numbers and call them yourself.

Choosing the numbers also allows Directors to give up an initial idea for a better one as they announce numbers. If the Director initially wants 3 characters for a restaurant scene but then see that the two first choices who have just stepped on stage are looking inspired with each other, a better directing idea may come to mind. At that point they might adapt and discard the third number before committing to using them all in the scene.

Awareness of the Players
Suggest a scene, for example: 'two people at a bus stop'. If the players don't look, inspired by this suggestion, immediately suggest another scene. "How about escaping from prison?" A good idea is one that inspires the actors, not an idea that happens to please the Director.

> » If you have an excellent idea please don't use it – unless the players need it. A Director may be having ideas every five seconds - and perhaps should be - but if ideas are not needed they'll be disruptive and you'll be directing too much. «
> *Keith Johnstone*

Variations and Practice
Depending on the availability and confidence level, some Maestros occasionally use just one Director. This is workable for seasoned Directors when all other variables are positive and the performers are in a good state.

A second variation for training Directors is to have an apprentice or 'Director in training' sit in a third chair beside the other directors. The apprentice might watch and take notes for themselves, never actually directing throughout the show or they might be asked if they would like to try directing a scene or two. If asking the apprentice to direct, do so quietly so they do not feel pressure to do well.

In training your Directors, the apprentice variation is useful. Workshops and practices are also beneficial to get the feel, timing and wisdom of directing.

The best training for an Impro Director is being in front of an audience and actually doing it.

Gorilla Theatre™ is a good place to work your skills before Maestro. Responsibility for one scene every 20 minutes or so is much easier than every scene throughout the show.

> » The perfect director is a zen master! «   *Simone Bonetti - Bologna, Italy*

Player Initiative

When the Director/Player relationship is out of balance, and players have been implicitly trained to wait for the Director's input, players can lose initiative to start scenes and will hold themselves back when they should be moving forward.

Before the show, encourage initiative in the performers by telling them that when they are called to the stage they might occasionally want to initiate their own scenes. The selected Improvisers might see each other and feel motivated to begin without suggestions. They might start a date, job interview etc., without waiting for direction. When this happens the Director's job becomes easier. The performers are already inspired and Directors can simply respond. We don't want the performers to self direct all the time but the danger with directed formats is that the improvisers lose initiative in scenes. Encourage them to take it.

Let the performers know before the show that if the self initiated scene looks like a mess in the first 15 seconds you might stop it and ask if they would like to re-start. Then you can suggest something different.

In cases where Directors habitually control the players from beginning to end of shows, the players begin to feel powerless. Some players rebel and blame the format as being too restrictive while others give in to the restrictions and approach the show as puppets, always waiting for the strings of decisions to be pulled by the Directors. Initiative issues are a shared concern for Directors and players.

Coup de Comedy Festival - Orange County, USA
by Joel Veenstra

Relationships

The easiest way to make something happen on stage is to suggest something that will alter the relationship between the characters. (Keith defines this 'dramatic action' as one person being changed by another). Finding ways to alter characters through their relationship is far less stressful than trying to find a good idea.

Good ideas don't exist in the abstract. Moving performers towards relationship makes a story more immediate and personal. Amazingly, we avoid deepening connections on stage all the time. If the performers are playing a master and servant in a castle, bring the relationship closer. "Tell your servant you've been watching him sleep at night." "Tell your master you have fallen in love with her." "Tell your servant that you are actually his father". And even with what might seem non-human relationships, bring the relationship closer. "The pigeon has a message around it's leg that you read". "The old picture on the wall is not random, it looks like you, your mother, your best friend". "One night when you pray, a voice answers you". The animal or the object is drawn closer in emotional connections.

» A suggestion that leaves the players cold should be instantly replaced by a second suggestion – or a third, or forth. The players are there to delight the audience – not to please the Directors. «

Keith Johnstone

> One of the things most similar to directing Maestro is the theory of Nudge. When a small suggestion turns the scene... it's magic! «
>
> Simone Bonetti - Bologna, Italy

Questions/Triggers to Inspire Performers

A good Director technique is to ask a question of the players before the scene like: What inspires you, what drives you crazy, what scares you? Then suggest a situation for exploring it.

Some Directors occasionally ask the players, "do you have anything?". This tends to happen towards the end of the game and is almost always asked before a solo scene.

Ask players what job they wanted when they were 5 then set them up to be in that occupation. Not only will they be inspired but the audience will take a special interest in watching a person doing something they honestly want. Remember to move the scene forward when the opportunities arise.

Ask them what pisses them off in the world then give them a chance to solve the problem. Rob Mitchelson from Loose Moose in Calgary exploded emotionally when recalling his problems with bureaucracy at City Hall. What honestly fires you up emotionally is more interesting than watching you pretend to find interest where there is none.

Ask questions that touch the performer on some emotional level. "Start the scene saying the thing you were thinking before you proposed to your spouse."

If as a Director, you have insight on the people you work with, it should not be too difficult to think from their perspective about what would inspire, challenge or engage them personally. Most of those ideas are the ones we want to put forward as Directors.

- "Can you play your son when he and his friends are talking about their parents?"
- "In a solo scene can you be your logic arguing with your libido at a bar."
- "Could you play your favourite/worst teacher showing how they changed you?"
- "Convince Death that you deserve one more day!" (might be a little heavy for some and not a great show opener but you know most people in the audience are asking themselves, "what would I do in that situation?")
- "Have a party with versions of yourself."
- "Travel back in time with a message for yourself."
- "Have the after-game interview by the sports network about your first kiss."
- "Do the scene you would like to have done with the boss who pushed you too far."
- "Be God in the heaven you run."

Over-directing

Over-directing is a common mistake and likely to happen if the Director knows how they would play the scene, or has a vision of how the scene should develop as if it was scripted. The empathy of a Director to place themself in the role of the performer and know how they might do the scene is a gift as long as that doesn't impede the judgement that the scene can happen in many ways.

Practice seeing through the performer's fear and confidence. You may not understand the choice of the performer but if they look confident with their choice, and the scene is doing well give them space to perform. If the players are experienced you may not need to direct a scene at all. If you direct when you don't need to you'll seem controlling and stifling. Heavy handed Directors who wish to be the star of Maestro don't inspire their partners by feeding them all the actions and lines. Few players enjoy playing out someone else's script for the entire night when they come to play freely. Do what you can to encourage players to trust their impulses, initiate their ideas and react without expectation of perpetual coaching.

Directors should resist the impulse to direct what an improviser is about to do or say. This is a temptation that Directors should resist. Be invisible when you aren't needed. Scenes can go in new directions if you let the improvisers venture outside of your ideas.

Det Andre Teatret
Oslo, Norway
by Kjetil Aavik

Det Andre Teatret, Oslo, Norway 📷 by Kjetil Aavik

Under-directing

When you are being too timid while the moment begs you to speak up, you will see the scene lose its focus and flounder around without purpose. In the note session after the show when you say "I thought about saying something but..." you know that you probably should have spoken. Letting a scene go down a destructive path for too long will make it much more difficult to salvage. At least if you pitch in, the pain is shared, even if you can't solve the problem. There is no science here but if you have a tendency to say, "I should have followed my impulse." then take more risks.

New Directors

When first directing, you might be looking for too much. New Directors feel like they have to see everything. That pressure creates stress. In response, your body releases a surge of cortisol and adrenaline. Your heart rate increases and blood pressure rises. Your brain narrows focus to fight or flight and your observation skills become limited.

That stress will blind you to what's important. When beginning as a Director, specialize in 2 or 3 of the most important elements of improvisation and look for them in the scenes. By looking for the minimum, your brain relaxes. The relaxed mind will catch more than those 2 or 3 things that you originally intended. Paradoxically by trying to do less, you will accomplish more.

Here are some simplified directing topics to watch for (at the beginning just pick one or two):
- Watch for negative beginning in scenes
- Watch for avoidance of relationship (move them towards relationship)
- Have them define when they avoid it.
- Have them react to things that any normal person would react to. "Go back and react strongly to the proposal, the gun, the ghost, the gift, the lie…"
- See offers the audience sees that the performers are missing.
- Make them fulfill promises. "I'm leaving you." "Leave!". "Pull a gun… Shoot it!" "I got you a gift." "Open it!". "Climb the mountain, enter the cave, kiss...."

Picnic Improvisación Teatral - Monkey Fest Bogota, Colombia by Fernanda Pineda

Summary of Directing Skills

Useful Impro skills related to directing include the following:
- awareness of the show needs
- awareness of performer limitations
- ability to inspire the performer
- willingness to react to the needs of a scene and the ability to dive into a difficult scene situation even when the director feels uncertain about what the right answer is (it can sometimes be better to do something and fail, than to do nothing and let your partners fail all by themselves)
- a good sense of how an audience is feeling and ability to filter out their surface desire loud calls for cheap humour or banal references
- ability to delay gratification and trust your partners on the stage (the performers)
- a balanced ego that allows performers to shine above your own ideas, opinions or artistic wishes
- an awareness of multiple narrative possibilities in any given moment
- the ability to release one's own ideas in favour of new directions

Directors develop their skills by doing. Direct in class, have workshops on directing, watch good Directors.

» As a Director your work is to remove the fear from players and give them the permission to take big risks on stage. «
Giuseppe Marchei, i Bugiardini, Rome, Italy

Useful Direction

Occasionally say... "Start a scene." or "Begin." (no suggestion)

See when inspiration has been ignored (one player looks at you while the other player looks at her). Say, "Notice that number 4 has already started the scene".

If improvisers are a little out of sync with each other, you can nudge them forward by clarifying what is going on. "Tina wants you to be her butler.", "Go to sleep so Gerald can be the tooth fairy and climb in your window."

Advance. You would be surprised at how easy it is to direct by simply saying, "move forward". Many improvisers delay the action because they are scared. (scared to define, scared to show emotion, scared to improvise). If poison is poured, it had better be consumed, and cause a strong reaction. If you've been standing at the entrance to a cave you had better go in. Listen to the audience whispers. You sometimes hear the voices, "kiss her" when the couple have shown the signals of what must happen. Move forward.

If someone says yes to a marriage proposal, cutting to the honeymoon is reasonable. If a chef remarks on how sharp a knife is, have someone impaled on it. This fear to move forward is especially true when it comes to dark, risky or taboo material. Improvisers, especially beginners, often shy away from material of this kind, but if the story is heading in that direction, don't be afraid to follow it there. If the story is dull and you can liven it up by adding a little spice, then do it.

Define. Watch performances and listen for words like 'things', 'stuff' and 'I don't know'. When the performer is scared to define, the scene can't move forward. Give the pet a name. Sebastian the Bull Mastiff, is much better than feeding 'the pet'. Climbing Mount Sinister implies a lot more than just climbing that generic mountain.

Move performers towards action rather than words. Having an improviser climb out on the window ledge is more interesting than an improviser telling his boss that he is depressed and angry about being fired. Illustrate rather than narrate.

Remember the practical stuff. Encourage loud, clear speaking. Encourage players to slow down if feeling a little nervous. Under stress, we talk too fast, speak too much and raise the pitch of our voice. Good suggestions to slow people down are to say things like "do the rest of the scene as if you are underwater". Directors should give players something constructive or creative to do rather than simply undoing or dismissing what is already going on.

As an experienced improviser/teacher/coach, your sense of the obvious should be quite well developed. You should know from past experience that what strikes you first tends to be the better choice. Be the one to keep the story on track and get the performers to justify peculiar choices when oddities arise, or go back and remove the odd choice.

Being obvious is meaningless unless context is considered, based on what the players have established already. Be careful you are not simply substituting your obvious for theirs. For example, imagine the audience suggests a scene about a pupil in detention. Your first thought might be for the pupil to be sexually precocious, but the improvisers quickly establish that the teacher envies the pupil's daring instead. Now the scene is not about sexuality and it is not helpful to have the players go back and use your idea instead.

*Grund Színház
Budapest, Hungary*
by Grund Színház

» The content should get better as the night goes on. «
Keith Johnstone

PLAYERS

Advice

Step on stage improvising.
Respond to your partner's striped shirt (taking pictures of the last zebra). Respond to your partner's smile. "I won't tell anyone about us if you don't...".
Commit yourself before the show to start ONE scene without Director's input.
Your inspiration is your strength. If you continually subjugate inspiration, you train yourself to ignore it in the future. By acting on inspiration you will most likely start a scene that you want to be in.
If the goal of the Director is to create an atmosphere that inspires you and the audience, then your initiative supports that vision.
The beauty of taking that first step in the scene is the support you give the Directors. They will feel less pressure to carry the entire show and with less stress might perform better in their roles. Additionally, your initiative gives Directors choices. They can choose to allow the scene to move forward because your choices support the needs of the show or they can stop the scene and restart one that will be better suited to the moment. You've doubled your chance for a good scene and improved the show.
When a scene finishes, players should clear the stage for the Emcee and avoid wasting time with post scene antics or emotion.

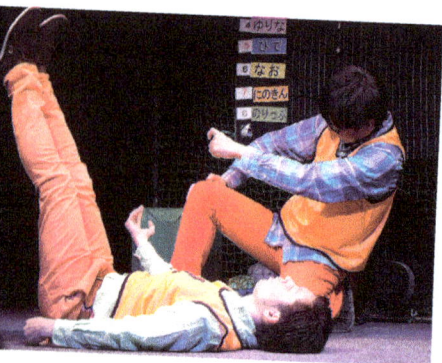

Impro Japan - Tokyo, Japan by Impro Japan

Behaviour/Misbehaviour

Your attitude on stage can add or detract from a Maestro show. This attitude is the same for all shows but consider the qualities of Maestro that are specifically reliant on your behaviour.
When scoring the scene, many audience members feel an initial hesitation to score low for scenes that deserve low scores. Some audience members have your emotional safety in mind. If you were to react hurt by a score of 1 out of 5, they would be less likely to score truthfully in the future when scenes deserve low scores. They would score everything a 3 or higher and Maestro would become artificial and disconnected from the audience's true feelings.
You train your audience to be honest by showing them that the scores do not actually hurt you. Some performers have taken great bows after low scores and announced with a smile "This audience does not truly understand art!". The audience in this case is reassured that the actor is uninjured because of their playful response, and feels more confident expressing what they feel. We don't want to see this behaviour after every scene but the spirit is a good one.
How you behave as the lights are coming down on your scene makes a big difference to the score. As the performer, you may have felt that the scene was not very good. When your disappointment is evident - head down and skulking off the stage like a deflated balloon - the audience is left with your opinion versus their own. They may have liked the scene, but they will score it lower because you have told them already that it was not worth their appreciation.
Conversely, have you ever been to a show where the improvisers are seriously praising themselves (overtly or otherwise) and you are thinking something very different? It shows a sign of disconnection to be overly proud of mediocre work in front of a paying audience. Let them judge. Enjoy what you do but find the appropriate level of self congratulation.
Player misbehaviour is a concept that comes up in Theatresports™ and Gorilla Theatre™. It has less function in Maestro. While misbehaviour is encouraged at some level in most of Keith's formats, be cautious that performers who are prone to misbehaviour don't draw focus from the structure.

Joining Scenes

Improvisers might enter into scenes they were not originally called into. They might have joined as an extra support character (the waiter in a restaurant) only to discover that their role has taken on a narrative significance. Or they might enter a scene but be thrown off by a Director who sees their involvement as a distraction.

When an improviser enters a scene after it has begun, he or she is not scored if they have already been scored in that round or if their role in the scene is just background to the narrative. If they have not performed and been scored in that round and their participation has significance to the scene, they are asked if they would like to be included in the score. If they say yes they will receive the score that the audience votes for. If the performer chooses not to be included in the scoring then they will stay eligible for another scene in that round. The dramatic moment the performer chooses to be included or not included in that scene's scoring is always fun to watch.

> » I love to play up the stakes of being involved in the scoring of a scene, or heightening the gamble of it but boldly saying something like, "Yes! I want to be included in the scoring on that scene, there's no way I can improvise something better on my own!", or "No - don't include me, I can do way better." If it's said with a twinkle in the eye, you can either win over an audience, or take on the role of 'misbehave-er' of the evening. «
> *Rebecca Northan - Loose Moose Theatre, Calgary / Spontaneous Theatre, Toronto, Canada*

ENDING THE GAME

If a show is running overtime, it is possible to simply declare whoever is leading in the score as the winner.
If the scores are tied or similar, there are several possibilities to determine the champion in a satisfying showdown. If needed, the audience votes for the one who succeeded technically as well as who helped the scene the most, or simply who they liked better. Here are some suggestions. Try out your own experiments to see what works.

Tie Breakers - between two people
- Hat Game - (best two out of three rounds) (see IMPRO FOR STORYTELLERS pg. 156-161)
- Most believable I Love You scene - (between trolls, in an elevator, at a library, etc) (IFST pg. 272-273)
- Happy low status - (IFST pg. 223-224)
- Happy high status - (IFST pg. 223-224)
- Leg Wrestling or other safe physical challenge
- Scene without letter S - three strikes you are out, strike for not taking risks or play a scene while scorekeeper keeps count of how many times people use the letter S and announce a winner (IFST pg. 188)
- Rhyming scene (IFST pg. 245-246)
- No questions, all questions
- (any 2-person scene can also work)

Tie Breakers - between three or more people
- Hat Game - (either starting a new scene with each elimination or continuing as the defeated player makes an excuse to leave when they lose their hat)
Blindfolded version of hat games is a favorite in some theatres (IFST pg. 160)
- Die Game/Story Story Die - with/without deaths - (when including the deaths keep them fun, short and with variation.) Some people misunderstand the 'deaths' in Die Games. After doing a verbal story game, it is good variation to have the physical work which in this case is usually a short bit of mime to contrast the talking. Of course no one wants to see a physical representation of people killing themselves so don't just mime a gun to your head or anything so blatant. If the audience sug-

gests, "Park Bench" then finish your lunch on the bench, lick the tasty food off your fingers then enjoy the taste of your fingers and continue until you have devoured yourself… We're not trying to do serious dieing scenes (especially at the end of the show). (IFST pg. 183-184)
· No S - (see above)
· Questions - (see above)
· Endowment in Gibberish - 90 seconds. (if one person is leading, the other two can compete to help the leader guess the job, relationship, situation/problem of the scene) The audience decides who will go on to the final tie breaker with the leader.
· Pecking Order (IMPRO pg. 67-70)

Solo scenes - (Audience votes for the one they liked more if you definitely need to end the show - otherwise you risk having players getting the same scores and being stuck in a tie)
· Dear Diary - (writing diary entries - Directors (or the player) say "next day" often to keep the scene moving forward in time)
· play all characters
· scene with a puppet/puppets
· Evil Voice - (a voice in inside you comes out)
· break up or first date - (play both roles or with your hand as a puppet)
· give a Ted Talk - (or similar speech - valedictorian, political speech)
· scenes with audience member
· break out of prison
· mime scenes, Advancing/Not Advancing - (with emotional sounds)
· live the life cycle of an animal chosen by the audience
· perform your life highlights from birth to death
· perform a favorite fairy tale / movie alone in a couple of minutes
· one end of a telephone conversation
· single play - What Comes Next (IFST pg. 141)
· song
· monologue explaining why the other finalist should be the Maestro
· (most Gorilla Theatre™ forfeits fit in here)

The Big If - Impro Festival Barcelona, Spain
📷 *by Riccardo Salamanna*

THE WINNER AND ENDING THE SHOW

Impro Japan Tokyo, Japan
📷 *by Impro Japan*

The end of the show is the exclamation point on what we hope was a fun evening full of variety and spontaneity. You probably want to continue the enthusiasm and pace after the final scene into that final moment when the lights come up on the audience and they leave your theatre with great memories and high feelings.

As soon as the winner is known, (whether it happens because of a tie breaker or just because the points show them as the Maestro Champ) the runner(s)-up are given a quick thank you and applause and then we focus on the winner to see if the audience thinks they deserve the prize.

The Maestro champion is likely the person the audience wants to be their winner. That person should be treated the way the audience would want to be treated themselves if they had won the show.

SAMPLE CLOSING

Emcee: "How about a hand for our runner-up (second place) Alfonso?"
(The second place player goes to the side and the prize is brought on.)
"Theresa is the Maestro champion but… there is one more task for the audience. You must decide whether or not she deserves this 5 dollar bill."
"All those who think Theresa does not deserve the 5 dollars, please clap now." (Wait for response) "Everyone who thinks she does deserve the prize, clap now."
The winner is given the prize and all of the eliminated players come on stage (to triumphant music) celebrating the Maestro's victory.
The winner accepts the prize and briefly address the audience, thanking them for coming, and wishing them a safe trip home. What the winner says should be short, positive and reflect the feeling you wish the audience to leave with.
Theresa: "Thanks for coming everyone. Don't forget about the other shows we offer here. See you next time!"

(Everybody waves, claps, celebrates and heads back/off stage.)
The rest of the performers should be supportive and enthusiastic about the winner and leave with the audience feeling that they know you are about to go off and have a fun celebratory party for The Maestro.

left:
Loose Moose Theatre
Calgary, Canada
by Kate Ware

Det Andre Teatret
Oslo, Norway
by Kjetil Aavik

» I consider the image of benevolence created by the losers congratulating the winner as the real ending of Maestro, and as the image that the spectators should take with them as they leave the Theatre. That's why we don't take a bow. What matters is seeing the winner being carried off in triumph and approval. « *Keith Johnstone*

THE PRIZE

If you place a truly amazing prize at stake, then the egoes of performers and even the wishes of the audience are skewed by the prize.
Traditionally, the Maestro prize is of little actual worth but the improvisers endow it with great importance. The prize should not be intentionally stupid or difficult for performers to give importance to. Very early in Maestro's development, the prize designated at the Loose Moose Theatre was a framed Canadian 5 dollar bill. It represented something but not enough to drive the performers to fight aggressively for it. The fancy frame around the bill added to the endowed value.

The Big If - Impro Festival
Barcelona, Spain
by Riccardo Salamanna

ATTENTION TO DETAIL

CONTENT

The content of your performance within the format is, of course subject to performer's skills and the artistic tastes and direction of your group. Keith Johnstone has consistently set about guiding his Maestro shows (and all other shows for that matter) away from purely light or superficial offerings. The desire is to move shows towards variety and connection with the audience that visits us. Memorable scenes from Maestro reflect memorable work from any show, improvised or traditional theatre. Here are some actual scenes from around the world:

- An epic battle with the spectre of death where the daughter offered herself for her father's safety only to discover the natural process of life could not be thwarted.
- The difficult talk of where babies come from that left the audience laughing minutes after the scene was done because of how uncomfortable the child had made the parent with graphic details of what sex was really about.
- What happens with politicians and big business in discussions behind the scenes of the Trans-mountain Pipeline in western Canada.
- Intergalactic mistakes reminiscent of earth's history with aboriginal cultures.
- Bed time for a young audience member based on his true story of befriending a house fly.

No structured games were incorporated in these particular scenes but in the shows where these scenes occurred there were also highly structured games like 'Yes Let's' and 'Word at a Time' as well as silly hoop games that balanced the show's need for chaos mixed with pathos and spectacle. Variety will engage your audience and encourage their return. Safe games played just for laughs will not aid in your development and eventually chase away all but new audience members.

Theatre Anundpfirsich
Zurich, Switzerland — *by Theatre Anundpfirsich*

IMPACT360
Osaka, Japan
by Takayuki Ueda

>> The key for a good Maestro is listen to the audience as if it's an actor on stage. <<
Simone Bonetti - Bologna, Italy

PERMISSION AND DIFFICULT CONTENT

At the time of writing, consent and content have become hot topics in the improvisation community, and society at large. We recognize that each company will find the best way to approach these topics as they see fit. By its nature, a Maestro cast is varied in skill level and experience, and may be unlikely to have developed personal connections between players. Some performers in the same show might not know each other at all. The level of safety and trust each person has, or their needs, will vary greatly between participants and companies. Therefore, we encourage you to discuss these topics openly and with an eye to a balanced understanding and mutual agreement on direction.

If your company has questions or wishes to engage an outside voice on the topic of consent and permission, please contact your ITI Regional Representative or the ITI office. (See Contacts at the end pg. 48)

Der Kaktus
Würzburg, Germany
by Nicolas Dreher

FAIRNESS

Some groups are immediately tempted to weaken elements of Maestro they view as unfair. They lessen the amount of elimination rounds or change the scoring so that winners and losers will be scored more similarly. This attempt at a fair show weakens the Maestro format and dampens the development of a company's improvisation. The arc of the show, which Maestro consistently and successfully encourages can be ruined by misguided attempts to flatten the highs and lows of the dramatic structure. The thrill of elimination, the risk of defeat and the struggle for victory all add to the drama for the audience.

On the surface Maestro can feel unfair. A beginner may get a higher score and stay in the game because he or she is in a scene with a more experienced player. The opposite can happen when an experienced player is eliminated early in the game because they were in a scene that was rated low. But this unpredictability is more rare than having the show propel its strongest players forward while releasing the less successful players of the evening. The drama of the underdog rising to the top, or the great improviser falling early adds to the drama of the night when it does occur.

It is always in the best interest of the Director to put forward the scene or game that would best support the audience and show throughout the evening. Great performers, whether they win the format or are eliminated immediately know that they are a part of the show and their elimination is a valid part of the audience's experience in the big picture.

Like other competitive Impro shows, the competition should be perceived by the audience as a game. It shouldn't feel seriously competitive. In the end it is not individual scores that matter but the quality of the show as a whole. Rather than focusing on the weaker argument that the competition is unfair, groups should keep an eye on the tendency for some performers who might focus too much on their ego and not enough on their scene partners and needs of the audience. The competition is for the audience. Letting one's ego step into the equation steals an important aspect of entertainment from those who have paid to see the performance.

TIPS

- Keep the show moving efficiently. The Emcee shouldn't take too many re-votes, players should leap on stage when called and Directors should not dither.
- Where props and scenography is available, players who are called up should not set the stage with props and furniture. They should allow the others to set up the office / bedroom / etc. for them while they attend to each other and to the director.
- Accept being eliminated with good nature. It will happen a lot. Make lots of mistakes and make them early. We learn quicker that way.
- If you feel a pre-show warm-up is necessary, keep it short. A warm-up is working if players are laughing and having fun.
- Players should remember that the show is more important than the success or failure of each individual scene. If a scene is in trouble, off stage players should consider helping whether to save the scene or find a merciful end. Likewise, if a scene is doing well, stay out and wait your turn.

There are horror stories where Maestro Directors have been given enormous, absurd thrones to sit on and made out to be the stars of the show, or companies where the most experienced players have all the power and want all the stage time and so make the most junior players direct. None of these actions work to support the nature of Maestro. It is better to make the Directors and direction unobtrusive. This helps keep focus on the players and scenework.

Grund Színház
Budapest, Hungary
by Grund Színház

PITFALLS

- Many groups misunderstand the role of Director and end up exploiting the improvisers. For example, one incarnation of Maestro has the Emcees or leaders of the show decide on games and scenes beforehand then request them in a predetermined order. They tell the improvisers what they must do, then provide no assistance to them. Many are game heavy and the result is a bit like a circus where one trained act follows another.
- In some groups, the hosts (Emcee) often dominate the show and highlight themselves rather than giving focus to the scene work.
- Some groups have blended the role of Emcee and Director. This is not advisable as neither job can be given the full focus needed by the person doing the job.
- There can be a problem of players being greedy for stage time. These players intrude in everyone else's scenes and destroy the efficiency of the show. Their actions and comments are mainly ways to get noticed throughout the show.
- Avoid players formally lining up on stage to receive scores from the audience. The message sent by doing this is that the performers themselves are involved in a judgement process. We want the audience to judge the scene and not the people.

SCENOGRAPHY

If you are fortunate enough to have your own space, a backstage area that allows you to accommodate large scenography (chairs, tables, beds, boats) and smaller hand props and costumes. This can add production value to the show and interactive possibilities for the performers. In an environment with sofas, tables and chairs moving on stage and off, concentrate on safety and accessibility. If you can't access it safely and efficiently in the show, then it doesn't serve you. And if it causes injury or creates concern in the audience's minds, it isn't worth using.

If you don't have access to a backstage, portable coat racks on the side of the stage are nice to have if you want to add costuming to your show. When the stage is lit, however, visible props and costumes shouldn't look cluttered.

When acting as 'sceneographers' try to create a reality for the actors and Directors. Two chairs isn't a set. But put out those same two chairs, stand beside them looking at your watch and it's a bus stop! Be inspiring rather than funny. Comedy will come from the tension of you taking great care with the realities you create, and the ease with which you can make them disappear. If the Director says "no thank you", take it away as quickly as possible without taking focus.

Impro Melbourne
Melbourne, Australia
by Carolyn Wagner

Loose Moose Theatre
Calgary, Canada
by Heather Smith

MUSIC

Musicians are used by many improvisation companies. Be careful that the limitations of your stage does not create too many physical restrictions by having a musician on stage with the performers. (Be careful about the safety of cords and expensive instruments near clumsy improvisers).

The work of musicians can be a directing influence affecting the stories and characters, for good or ill. A strong musician chooses the right moments to support or enhance a scene. They can motivate improvisers who are tentative to feel deeply emotion still lingering on the surface. They can provide support or even contrast to atmospheric feeling or tension of the story. Skillful musicians both respond to the players/characters and make offers for them to respond to. Where the range of a musician's performing style is limited, the tone of the show can become limited as well. Shows that have a constant bed of sound with a similar feeling will destroy variety faster than a Director constantly telling the performers to always be sad or always be excited. One of the most useful skills a musician has is the ability to be silent. While the oblivious musician can unwittingly set the show down a path of monotony, a musician with the understanding of their influence on the show can use their talents to enhance variety.

Theatre Anundpfirsich - Zurich, Switzerland
by Mike Hamm

LIGHTS AND SOUND

Maestro benefits from good sound and lighting improvisers. As with musicians, their location should not impede the performers or create a perception of danger. While most groups focus exclusively on either a musician or a recorded sound technician, some groups effectively integrate both at the same time. Both the light and sound improvisers should be encouraged to take chances and make mistakes.

» We play in what was a movie theater. There is a grand piano on stage and a small drum kit. We always play with a live band. On the screen behind us the man running lights is also projecting images behind the scenes whenever appropriate, anywhere from 2 to 5 times per show. Usually to great effect. «
Andrew Hefler - Grund Színház, Budapest, Hungary

IN CLOSING

NOTES

Take about ten minutes for notes after the performance. You can achieve this by going through the Scorekeeper's list of scenes, mentioning whatever needs to be mentioned (music too loud over dialogue in love-scene, too much noise backstage in the hospital scene., etc.) If such snags aren't mentioned they occur week after week. The group should agree that notes are not the time for discussion, or everyone will have to have their say and notes will last for hours. Congratulate players who take the risks you want. Comments are more constructive and have less potential for hurt when they are directed towards the scene work and away from individuals. Attempt to give and receive notes with humility, understanding and detachment.

FINAL THOUGHTS

Picnic Improvisación Teatral - Monkey Fest - Bogota, Colombia by Fernanda Pineda

Maestro, played as intended, is one of the most consistently successful Impro show formats. It may be that the finalists are the most gifted players or they may be newcomers having an inspired night of improvisation. Even on nights when the scene work has not been remarkable it still seems like justice has been served when the brightest improviser keeps shining till the end and they are finally rewarded. The audience feels that their opinions and preferences matter as they influence the outcome of the night with their choices. We expect a few failed scenes, a few spectacular ones (the spectacular ones preferably near the end) and a lot of positive energy generated by happy people (players and audience) who are all involved in the experience together.

》On a good night, the audience is very invested in the competition, but doesn't care overmuch who wins.《
Tom Salinsky - The Spontaneity Shop, London, England

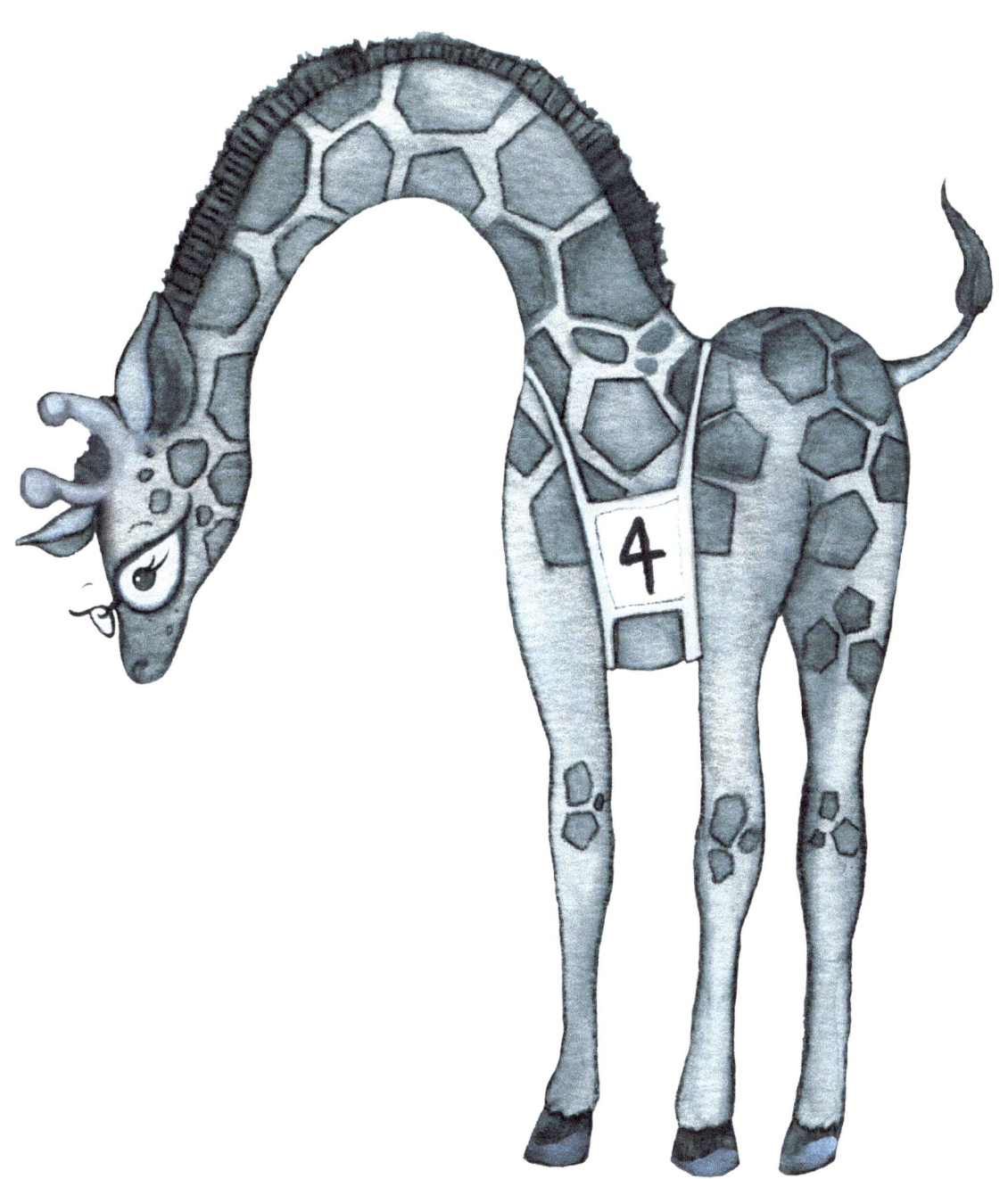

MAESTRO MEMORIES

» Italian improviser Tania Mattei performing at the final show of an Impro Intensive won the Maestro without speaking a word of english in front of an english speaking audience. «
Dennis Cahill - Loose Moose Theatre, Calgary, Canada

» I remember when Keith returned from a trip overseas... He briefed us on the mechanics of this new form he was calling Mice-tro (building on 'Gorilla'), taught it to us in an hour class and we performed it that night. «
Jeff Gladstone, Loose Moose Theatre, Calgary / Vancouver Theatresports, Canada

» In 2010, Keith came to Austin. He was generous enough to direct a Maestro. We rented the local Arts Center theater and had a packed crowd of over 200. In one of the final scenes, a solo scene, Keith told an improviser to "seduce the audience". The player (Troy Miller) arrogantly swaggered onto the stage and just calmly gestured towards his crotch with an "Eh?!" expression on his face. Keith pulled the lights. When the Emcee stood up to score the scene and asked "Was that scene a 1?" the entire audience joyously *erupted*, in unison. They were united and completely in on the joke of how intentionally bad the seduction was. Even though it was a "low score", it was the best-scoring moment for that show (and ever, in my opinion). That bit of improv united the entire audience of strangers. *That* is why we play Maestro. «
Kareem Badr – Hideout Theatre, Austin, Texas

» Like at many international festivals we had a Maestro with several guests. Alvan from Canada was in a scene where they spoke spanish. They were camping and got visited by a furious bear. Victor and Eli seemed to know what to do and could save themselves. Alvan got attacked and screamed "Aprender!!!!", believing he was calling for help. The bear grabbed him and disappeared with him in the forest. After the scene he found out that 'aprender' means 'learn'. So the message is pretty clear: Learn spanish so you don't get eaten by a bear. «
Luisa Winkler · Der Kaktus, Würzburg, Germany / The Big IF - Barcelona, Spain

» I remember during a lightning round, two Norwegian improvisers immediately became old people going somewhere in a hurry (very slowly). They were happy but we weren't sure what was going on. Then the one who was behind touched the other on the shoulder and shouted "Tag!". They both turned around (very slowly) and the chase began anew. «
Steve Jarand - Loose Moose Theatre, Calgary, Canada

»At the 'Würzburger Improtheaterfestival' 2018 the final two players were asked to sing a song together but they were having trouble with the microphones. While working out if the mics were 'on', the song had already started. They integrated what was happening in the moment and the song became a beautifully collaborative and positive duet about everything that is 'on'… their clothes, the lights, love… When it was over, the audience refused to declare one as the winner over the other. The directors resisted changing the regular outcome of the show until the audience began chanting "Break the rules!". In the end the revolution was successful and both ladies were crowned 'Maestro'. «

Kati Schweitzer, Impro Stuttgart / Der Kaktus, Würzburg, Germany

» My favourite Maestro of all time included a Yorkshire Terrier as one of the players. It was at Loose Moose, and we were a bit short on players that night. A long time, experienced player, Zackary Quinn, had her dog Chloe with her that night. We put a number on her, and she was called up in scene like everyone else. Not something I'd recommend doing on a regular basis, but great as something very special! Chloe was an exceptionally well trained dog - I think all of her scenes got '5s', and she made it through to the final round. Very humbling for all of us! «

Rebecca Northan - Loose Moose Theatre, Calgary / Spontaneous Theatre, Toronto, Canada

» We were near the end and needed to eliminate 2 or 3 players but there were 5 with the same score. Because of time, I had players pair up and play rock/paper/scissors where the loser is immediately eliminated and the winners are saved. The fifth player had no one to pair up with and I noticed that a little girl in the audience had been vocal in the show earlier so I offered her to play. By chance or because the player was skilled, the little girl won. I asked the girl, who was maybe 5 years old, if she wanted to play the rest of the Maestro (I asked the parents too if they were ok). She said yes and the audience roared and was so supportive of her. She ended up doing a scene with two other people where she was a pirate captain and the others were her shipmates, and a solo scene where I had her put another player to sleep by telling him a bedtime story and the other players acted it out in the background. She ended up winning (of course) and it was a lovely evening. «

Ian Parizot - Again! Productions, Paris, France

» I never won. Except once. And I remember that the day I won, I had volunteered to vacuum the stage. So I volunteered to vacuum the stage every day for months afterwards. «

Jeff Gladstone - Loose Moose Theatre, Calgary / Vancouver Theatresports, Canada

» In Würzburg, Germany, an unprecedented 6 was given when an audience overwhelmingly and spontaneously chanted for the higher score until it was granted to a Swedish solo scene. «

Shawn Kinley - Loose Moose Theatre, Calgary, Canada

7
IN CLOSING

RESOURCES

Keith Johnstone's Books
- IMPRO Improvisation and the Theatre
- IMPRO For STORYTELLERS - Chapter 3, pages 49-54
- keithjohnstone.com/writing
- impro.global/resources/publications/books

Keith Johnstone's Newsletters
- Micetro Impro 1990
- Gorilla and Micetro November 1998
- Newsletters are available through the ITI

DVDs
- Impro Transformations
- Trance Masks
- keithjohnstone.com/video

Workshops & Training
- Keith Johnstone Impro Intensives
- keithjohnstone.com
- Loose Moose Theatre International Summer School
- loosemoose.com
- ITI teacher list: impro.global

ITI Theatresports™ and Gorilla Theatre™ Format Guides
Available through all major book distributors

Biographical Information
Keith Johnstone - A Critical Biography by Theresa Robbins Dudeck
Questions about the "Keith Johnstone Papers" or inquiries about Johnstone's literary works, contact Theresa Robbins Dudeck, Literary Executor for Keith Johnstone
theimprofessor.com/contact

Impro Melbourne - Melbourne, Australia by Impro Melbourne

ITI Contact Information
Office: admin@theatresports.org
Regional Representatives: impro.global

APPENDIX 1

As an extension of the Skills section, Shawn Kinley describes the danger of misinterpreting skills using the concept of 'Accepting'...

It's important to learn and relearn even basic skills to allow you to see deeply into the work. Some improvisation groups may feel satisfied with having learned oversimplified explanations of improvisation techniques. For example:
'Always say yes! Never say no!'.
First, understand that the suggestion to say YES, and to ACCEPT is key to overcoming ingrained tendencies which kill good improvisation. We learn to accept ideas because we've been taught most of our lives to employ safety mechanisms which make us negate and control. We say 'No' even when there's no reason, as a reflex. This gets in the way of improvisers. So, we are taught SAY YES!!!! ACCEPT EVERYTHING!!!

While accepting offers is key to good Impro, saying yes to everything misses the actual point. Some improvisation groups understand this concept while others make YES a hard rule.

'The cult of YES' occurs when accepting moves to an extreme. Saying YES without thought becomes an unbreakable rule leading to performers who agree artificially regardless of truth and authenticity and to audiences who feel distant from the work on stage. Why would they want to come back?

Now, back to the ingrained tendency which is for most people to stay in control.
"Jump off that building!" "NO."
The protection serves you well in life. On stage, however, it inhibits forward movement. We want to move forward but that tendency to control and self-protect, kills ideas needlessly.
"Can I get you some Tea?" "No, I want Coffee."
Even with an idea that poses no risk, we might feel compelled to negate. That controlling behaviour delays us moving forward but gives the naysayer a weak sense of being in charge. Little do they know however, they are denying themselves and their partners a chance to move forward into adventure, connection and possibly some fun. The audience senses the difference and they sit back with crossed arms waiting for simple agreement and for the scene to move forward.
"Coffee?"
"Thanks."
"No problem. How's your superhero training going?"
"Great, thanks for asking. I can jump off of buildings and land now."
So things are moving forward….
At this point the lesson to say Yes, and to accept works well. Then things go too far and the Cult of YES creeps in. The danger is that saying yes as a rule to everything now negates the logic of the scene and the desires of the audience.
"I hear you are leaving superhero school."
"Ahh… yes… I thought I would open a coffee shop."
"Oh… yeah? That's good."
"OK. Goodbye."
"Yes." Is that the end of our adventure?
"Yes."
"Want some coffee?"
"YES."
"I'm gonna jump off the building now."
"YES!"
By saying yes to everything all the time, we end up agreeing to any stupidity because we believe that makes us good improvisers. That oversimplification has not helped us.
This is one example of good ideas being misunderstood. If we are smart enough, we do not allow what we've learned in the past to get in the way of learning better skills.
Misinterpretation of Keith Johnstone's work has lead some groups down paths of over-simplification. The history of the Theatresports format is testament to to great ideas being watered down by some people without fully understanding the idea in the first place.
To see a good example of where Keith himself finds reasons to block some ideas, practice the exercise "What Comes Next" where the player can say "NOPE" when not inspired by a suggestion. The scene work that comes from selective negating teaches storytelling that focuses on inspiring your partner. BUT… with all of this remember why we are taught to relearn to say YES in the first place and when NO is relevant.

APPENDIX 2

The following is an excerpt from The Improv Handbook - by Tom Salinsky and Deborah Frances-White.

How to be directed

For some improvisers, especially those introduced to the concept of directing and side-coaching later in their careers, having a director there who can tell them what to do threatens their identity as creative individuals–and, more important, as ostentatiously creative individuals. They want to be seen as entirely responsible for the choices they make on the stage. While understandable from a psychological point of view (fear and ego), this is a little peculiar set in the context of theatre in general and improvisation in particular.

Most improvisers understand this, and have no problem with 'yes anding' offers of any kind. So... if you are happy to be endowed with being my mother if I'm onstage with you, why are you complaining so bitterly about being instructed to play another improviser's mother by me when I'm sitting at the side of the stage or in the front row?

Well, comes the retort, for the same reason that you told me not to block the offer: It yanks the audience out of the story. Ah, well that poses a new question then doesn't it? The problem is not that I'm directing you, it's that my direction is calling attention to itself. What if I were a narrator? Then I'd still be adding information to the scene which you would have to accept, but you wouldn't object to that, would you? You're right, good direction does not call attention to itself, as we've discussed, but you have your part to play in that, too. If a director gives you an instruction, do it. If a director gives you a line of dialogue to say, say it. Don't wait. Don't contemplate. Don't work up to it. Do it. Say it right away and say it word for word.

Improvisers who feel that a director threatens the audience's perception of them as independently creative will often rewrite lines the directors give them.
Him: Angie, what are you doing here?
Her: Oh, er... I...
Director: Say "I'm pregnant."
Her: Tony, the thing is... I think I'm... going to have a baby. All the audience can think of now is "Why didn't she say 'I'm pregnant'?" Rewriting the line (you wouldn't feel you had to paraphrase every line of The Crucible, would you?) only draws further attention to the fact that you were directed to say something. If a director gives you a potentially funny line and you say it straight away, word for word, then you will get the laugh. It's funny if the character says it in context because then, and only then, it's part of the story.

Some improvisers make matters even worse...
Him: Angie, what are you doing here?
Her: Oh, er... I...
Director: Say "I'm pregnant."
Her: (To director) I was just going to. (To him) Tony, the thing is... I think I'm... going to have a baby.

If the director gives you something to do which you were about to do anyway, then various possibilities exist.
· Everyone knew you were about to do it, and you had been "about to do it" for a while and needed a push.
· You and the director are so in sync that the same idea occurred to you both at the same moment. Clearly, this is a very good thing indeed, and no cause for complaint.
· The director is padding their part and interfering unnecessarily.

> »If every scene is directed, something is wrong. Directors should keep a low profile. They only do what is needed. If the actors are doing fine - leave them alone. We display the performers not the Directors.«
> *Keith Johnstone*

Even in this last case, complaining about it on stage in front of the audience doesn't solve the problem (although it might be the beginning of an entertaining feud in a Gorilla Theatre™ show), and in the first two cases there is no problem. If you really feel that the director is getting in your way, then have them replaced or omitted and see if the audience enjoys the show more without them. The only way to find out if something works is to try it.

APPENDIX 3

Here is Rebecca Northan's account of gathering items for a Maestro show in a temporary location.

I was teaching a five-day Impro intensive to culminate in a Maestro with the participants. Starting from scratch, I was able to put a Maestro Kit together in 2 days, for just under $150, with elements purchased at my local secondhand shop, stationary & hardware stores.

[1] With no time to make buttons or pinnies, these name tags from a stationary store are large enough for our venue, and the clips won't damage clothing.

[2] Two matching tin plant holders from a secondhand store, and some large metal washers from a hardware store will give the right sound when Directors are pulling numbers.

[3] I found this trophy for $3.00 in a secondhand shop… Our Maestro will also receive $5.00 Canadian dollars… but they are not allowed to keep the trophy - it's symbolic only!

[4] The biggest cost was a magnetic white board ($115.00 CAD). Being short on time, I created a grid with black tape, left space for players to write their names with dry erase markers, and put numbers on plastic magnets that can move across the board as points are accumulated. I still need to put the rest of the 'tick marks' between the larger numbers.

Det Andre Teatret - Oslo, Norway 📷 *by Kjetil Aavik*

www.ingramcontent.com/pod-product-compliance
Lightning Source LLC
Chambersburg PA
CBHW061155010526
44118CB00027B/2978